The Lone Haranguer Rides Again

Brant Parker and Johnny Hart

CORONET BOOKS
Hodder and Stoughton

Copyright © 1975 by Field Newspaper Syndicate
Copyright © 1982 by Field Enterprises, Inc.

First published in the United States of
America 1982 by Fawcett Gold Medal
Ballantine edition 1983

Coronet edition 1984

British Library C.I.P.

Parker, Brant
    Wizard of Id : the lone haranguer rides again.
    I. Title   II. Hart, Johnny
    741.5'973   PN6728.W5

    ISBN 0-340-35646-4

_The characters and situations in this book are
entirely imaginary and bear no relation to any real
person or actual happening_

Printed and bound in Great Britain for
Hodder and Stoughton Paperbacks, a
division of Hodder and Stoughton Ltd.,
Mill Road, Dunton Green, Sevenoaks,
Kent (Editorial Office: 47 Bedford
Square, London, WC1 3DP) by
Cox & Wyman Ltd., Reading

6-13

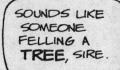

6·18

GALOOP
GALOOP
GALOOP
GALOOP
GALOOP
GALOOP
GALOOP
GALOOP
GALOOP

SWISH

THE KING IS A FINK

3-4

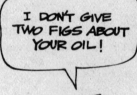

3-10

3-15

3-18

3-27

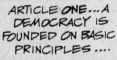

4-8

5-8

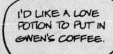

5-9

5-17

5.26

5-27

6·27

6-28

7·2

7-7

7-8

I THOUGHT YOU SAID YOU HAD A 100-FOOT POOL?

TRY TO TOUCH BOTTOM

7-9

7·11

7-15

7-16

7-21

7-24

THE CUCKOO IS BROKE

HE HAS TO MAKE HIS PAYMENTS JUST THE SAME

8-26

8·30